THIS JOURNAL BELONGS TO:

IF FOUND PLEASE CONTACT:

FREE DANCE LESSON FOR RETURNED JOURNAL!

Dear Dancer,

Self-love is a life-long commitment, and we are so proud of you for taking the time to nurture your spirit and mind. It is never too early or too late to begin this journey. Journaling has always been an integral part of our journey; we have found it to be therapeutic, enlightening and fun. We believe that dancers are magical and when we tap into our magic fully, anything becomes possible. As dancers, we focus on training our bodies so much that sometimes we forget to care for our mental health in the same way. We have to take care of ourselves in every way.

This 12-week guided journal will inspire you to reflect, dream and grow. We have experienced incredible success in our careers in film, television and live shows, but our greatest success has been that we have stayed healthy, happy, and true to ourselves! We want the same for you - the exercises in this journal are tools that we have utilized and continue to use to help guide us. We are so excited to be journaling, dancing, and connecting with you along the way!

Love, Chloë + Maud ♡

How this JOURNAL works!

5, 6, 7, 8... Let's Get Started!

Each week focuses on a specific theme which includes a writing prompt, a song to dance to, and a social media activity to complete. (If you do not use social media, please share your video with family and friends.)

At the beginning of each week, scan the **QR code** for an on-theme interactive video with Chloé and Maud.

Please use the hashtag #morethanmoveswithchloeandmaud and tag @chloeandmaud on Instagram and Tiktok.

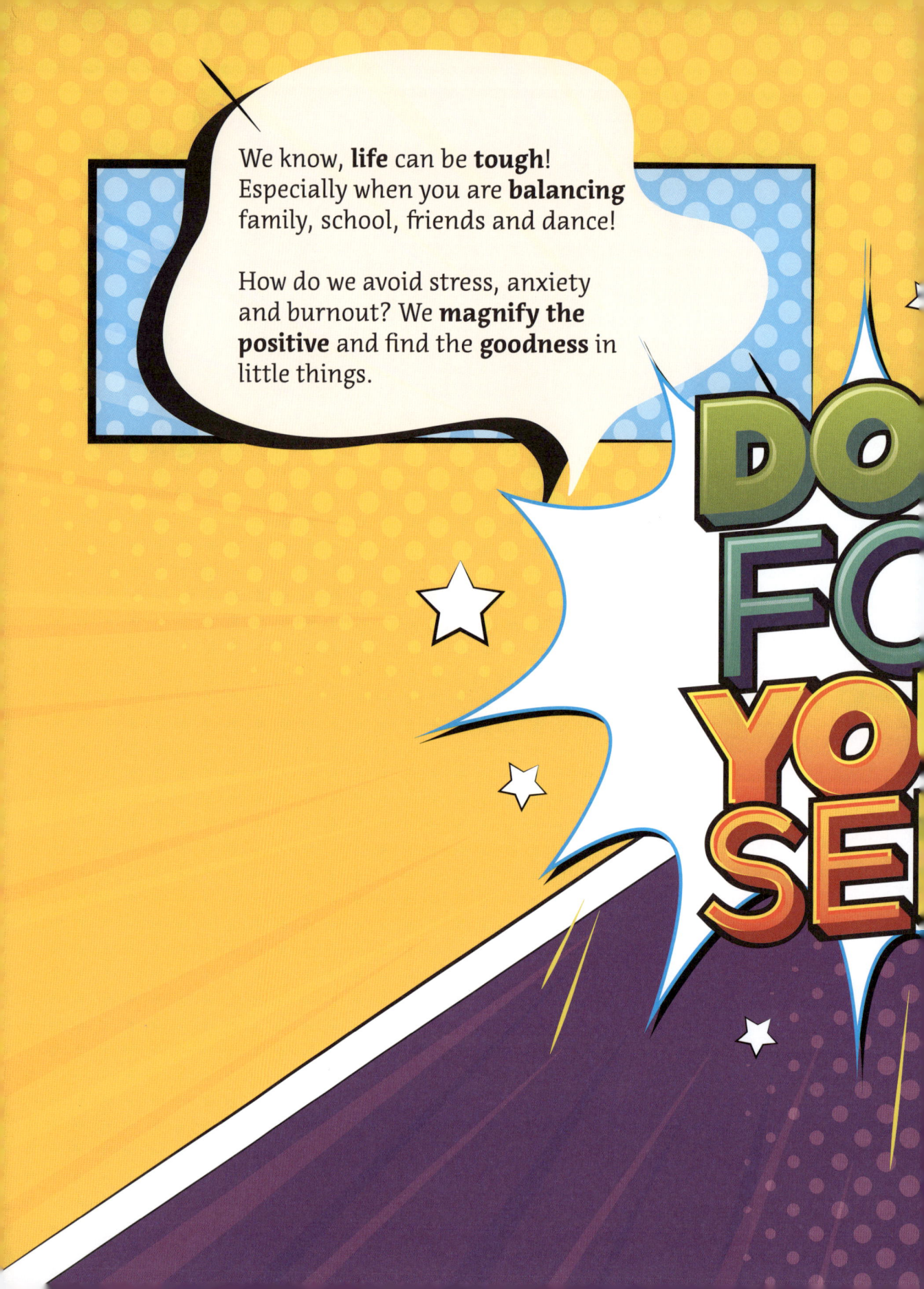

We know, **life** can be **tough**! Especially when you are **balancing** family, school, friends and dance!

How do we avoid stress, anxiety and burnout? We **magnify the positive** and find the **goodness** in little things.

On the **next page** write a **letter to your future self** in 12 weeks. As you write, ask:

What are you **hoping** to get out of this journal, and what **improvements** in yourself would you like to see?

How do you want to **feel**? Do you have any **goals** you want to **achieve** in the next 12 weeks?

At the **completion** of this journal, you will be able to **revisit** this letter and see how much you've **grown**!

Dear me...

Week 1
GRATITUDE

Lovely Day
Bill Withers

"MAGnify the POSITIVE!"
—Chloé

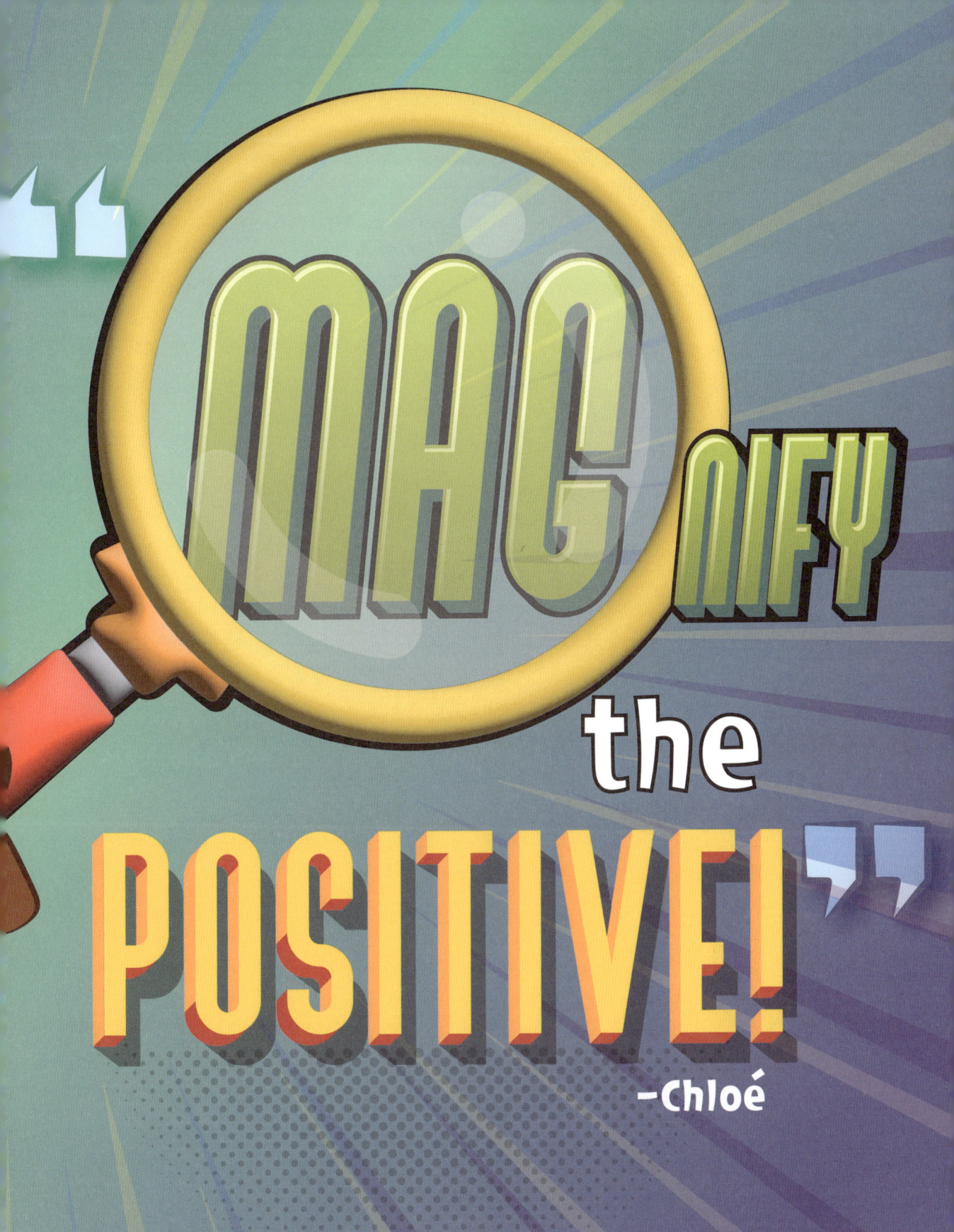

I am **Thankful** for:

It is easy to get **distracted** by the things that get us **down**. When we **reflect** on what we are **thankful** for life, **immediately** improves!

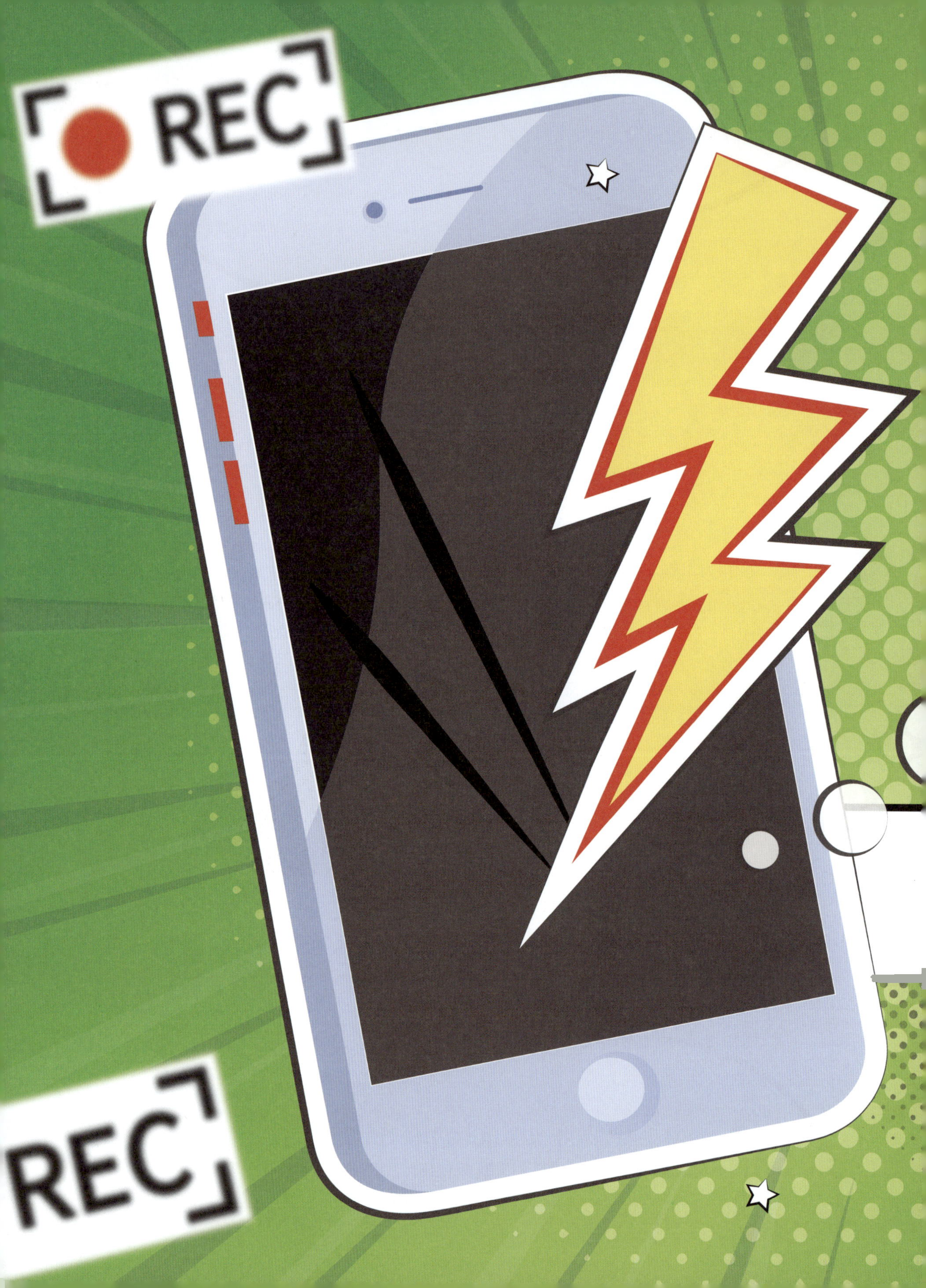
REC
REC

TIME to RECORD

Create a **video** on **social media** sharing things you are **grateful** for. You can read your list from the previous page or make it as **creative** as you want! This should be **fun** and stress-free!

MUSINGS INSPIRATIONS AFFIRMAT

ONS IDEAS QUESTIONS REFLECTIONS

MUSINGS INSPIRATIONS AFFIRMAT

ONS IDEAS QUESTIONS REFLECTIONS

Week 2

"SELF-

is recognizing and

HUMANIT

LOVE

celebrating your own

Y!"

"i"
Kendrick Lamar

Practicing self-love makes your life more joyful, purposeful and free. Self-love is a lifelong journey!

Things I love about myself:

THERE is ONLY ONE YOU!

I will **practice** self-love **every day** by:

AFFIRMATIONS

I promise to be kind to myself.

I promise to speak to myself with love.

"I Lo

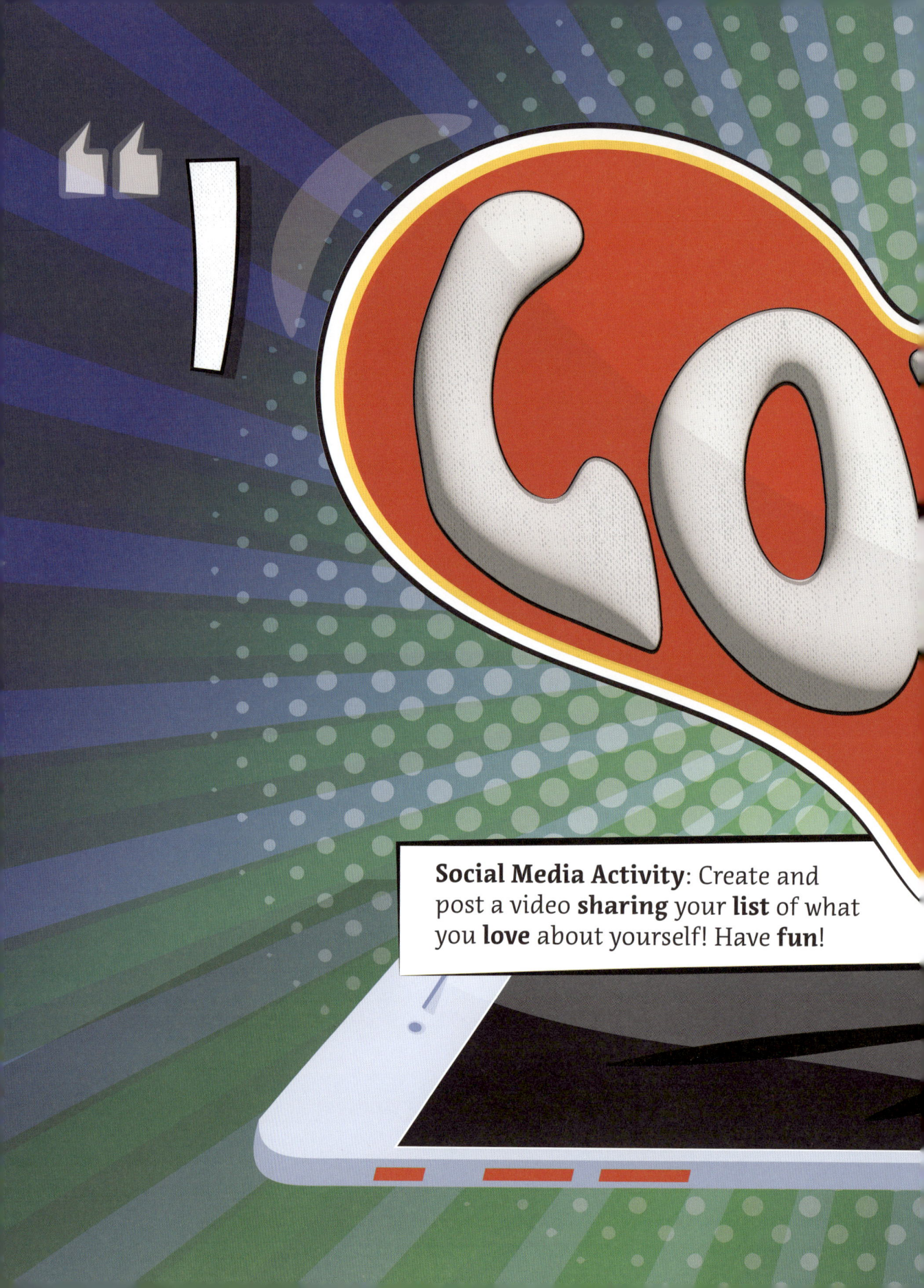

Social Media Activity: Create and post a video **sharing** your **list** of what you **love** about yourself! Have **fun**!

VE MYSELF!"

MUSINGS INSPIRATIONS AFFIRMAT

NS IDEAS QUESTIONS REFLECTIONS

MUSINGS INSPIRATIONS AFFIRMAT

NS IDEAS QUESTIONS REFLECTIONS

Week 3

"**JOY** IS HOW I MEASURE MY **SUCCESS!**

—Maud

Happy
Pharrell Williams

TIME TO MAUDIFY

Mau.di.fy: verb.
To see, be, and **create joy**!

We all **deserve** to have **joy** in our lives!
It is important to be **purposeful** in creating, seeking and sharing **joy**.

We **MAUDIFY** everyday!

People who bring me **JOY**:

Activities that bring me **JOY**:

Songs that bring me **JOY**:

Social Media Activity: Dance to a song of your **choice** that brings you **joy** and **explain** why this song makes you **happy**!

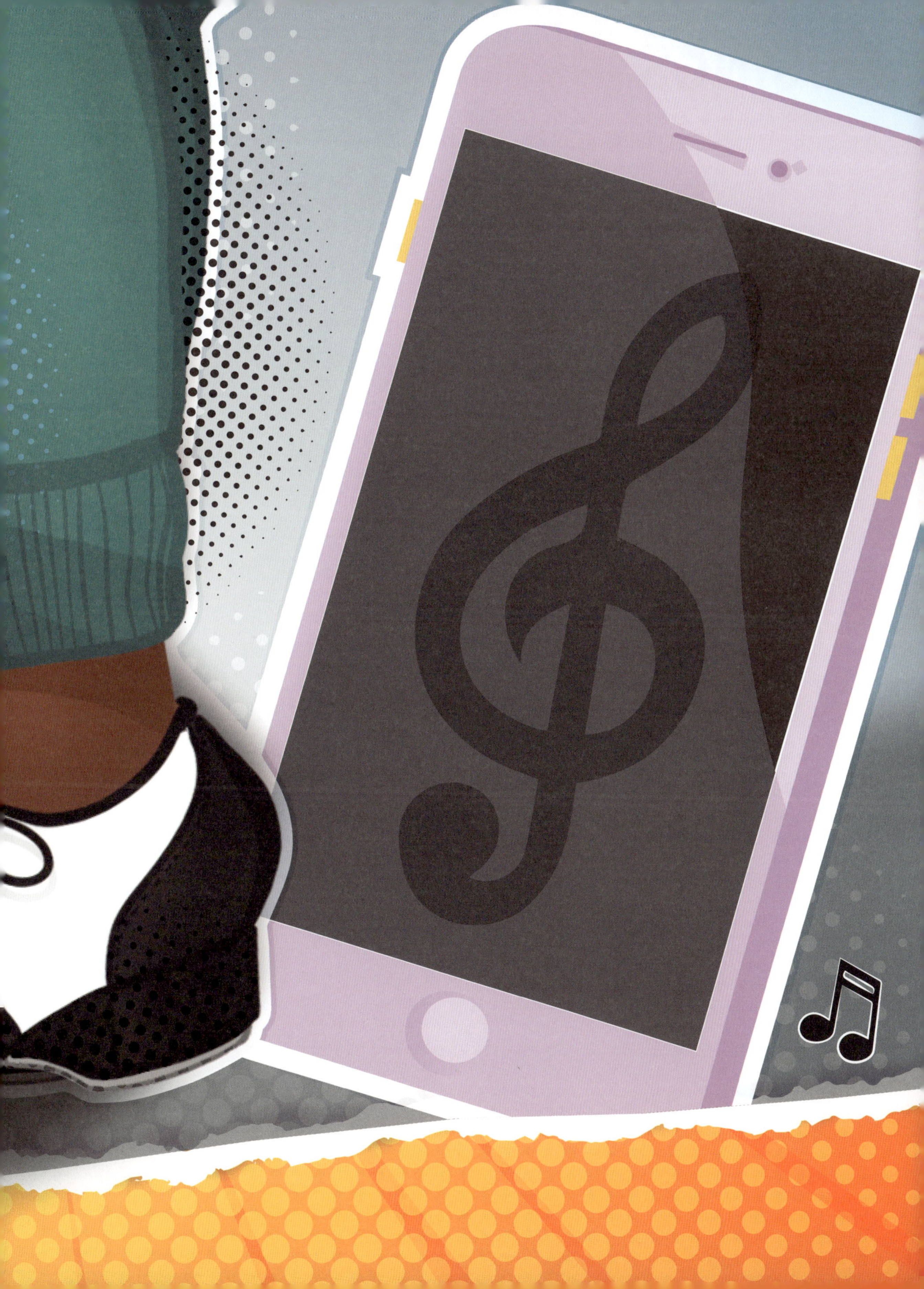

MUSINGS INSPIRATIONS AFFIRMAT

ONS IDEAS QUESTIONS REFLECTIONS

MUSINGS INSPIRATIONS AFFIRMAT

NS IDEAS QUESTIONS REFLECTIONS

Week 4

FRIENDS

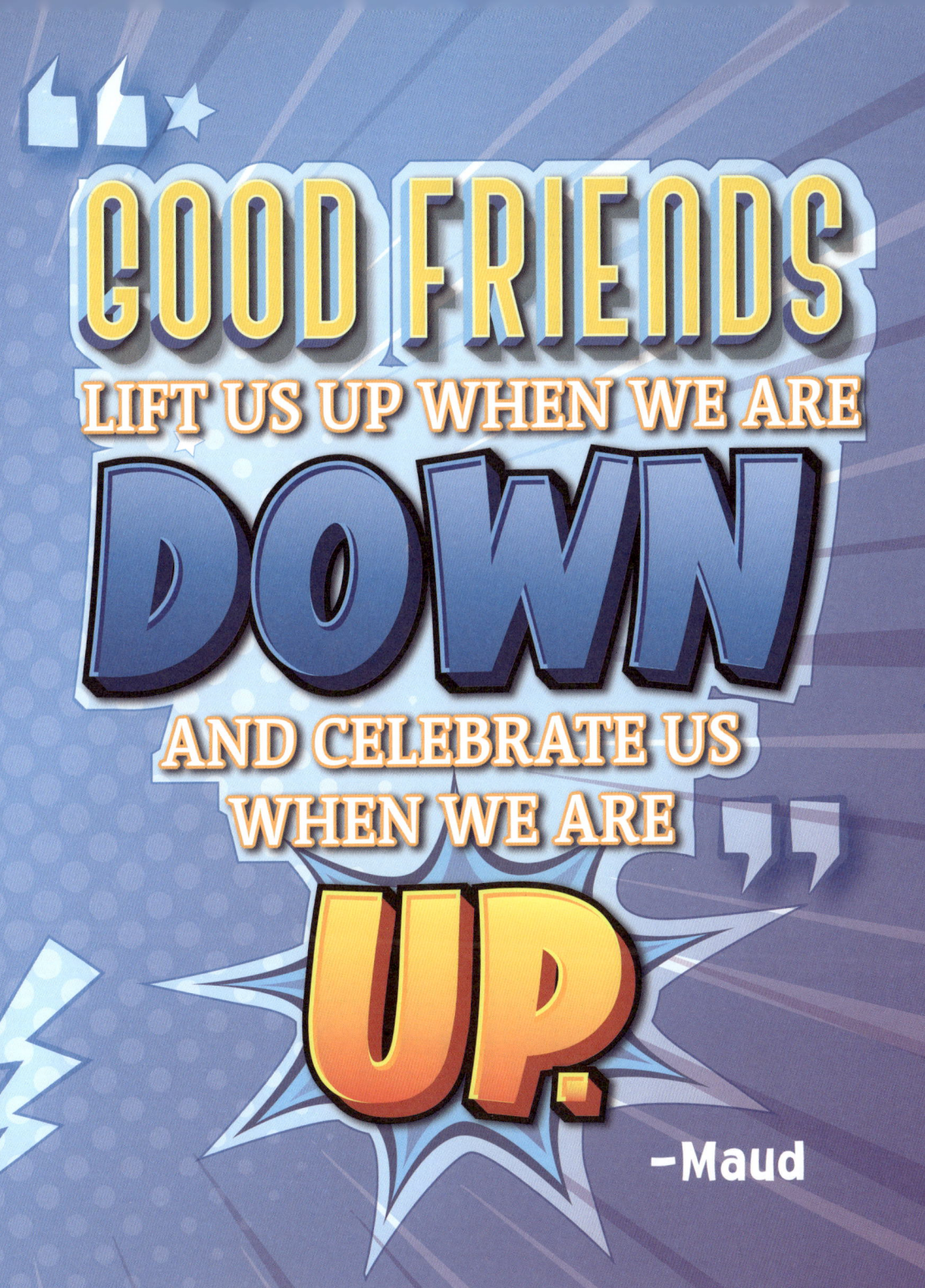

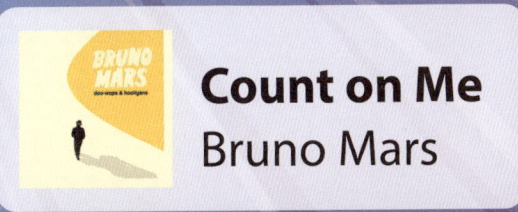

"**GOOD FRIENDS** LIFT US UP WHEN WE ARE **DOWN** AND CELEBRATE US WHEN WE ARE **UP.**"

—Maud

Count on Me
Bruno Mars

Your Squad is a reflection of you...

#SQUAD GOALS

Choose wisely!

Who you surround **yourself** with is **KEY**!

What **qualities** make a great **friend**?

List your **friends** who have those great **qualities**!

CELEBRATE FRIENDS

Social Media Activity: Celebrate one of your **amazing friends**! **Dance** with them if you can!

MUSINGS INSPIRATIONS AFFIRMAT

NS IDEAS QUESTIONS REFLECTIONS

MUSINGS INSPIRATIONS AFFIRMAT

NS IDEAS QUESTIONS REFLECTIONS

Week 5

Will
Joyner Lucas

"Seek guidance from those you trust!"

RSHIP

"Mentors are a guiding force, inspiration, & sounding board!"
—Maud

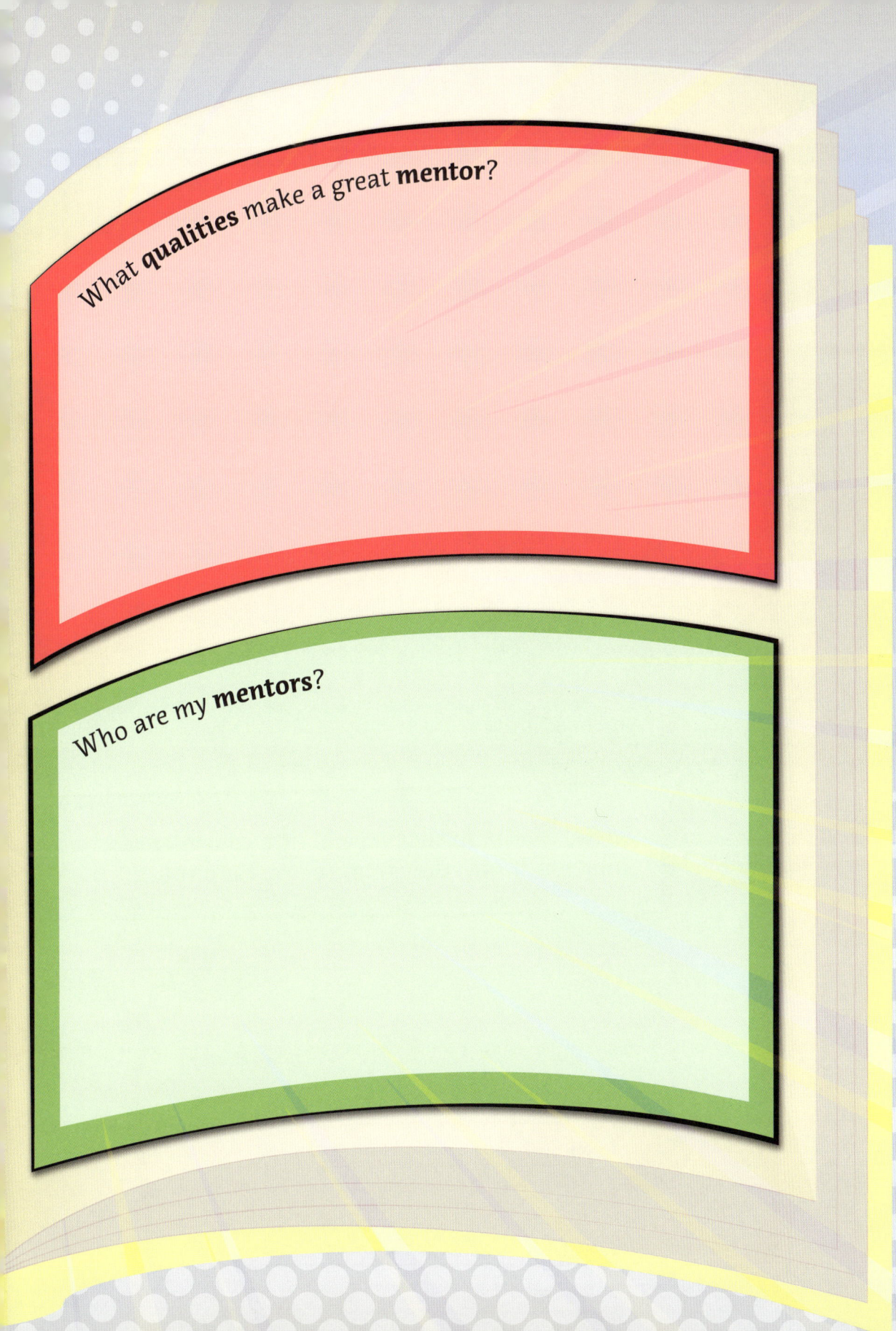

What **qualities** make a great **mentor**?

Who are my **mentors**?

CELEBRATE YOUR MENTOR

Social Media Activity: Celebrate your **mentor**. Talk about how they **inspire** and **help** you!

RATE

MUSINGS INSPIRATIONS AFFIRMAT

ONS IDEAS QUESTIONS REFLECTIONS

MUSINGS INSPIRATIONS AFFIRMAT

ONS IDEAS QUESTIONS REFLECTIONS

Week 6

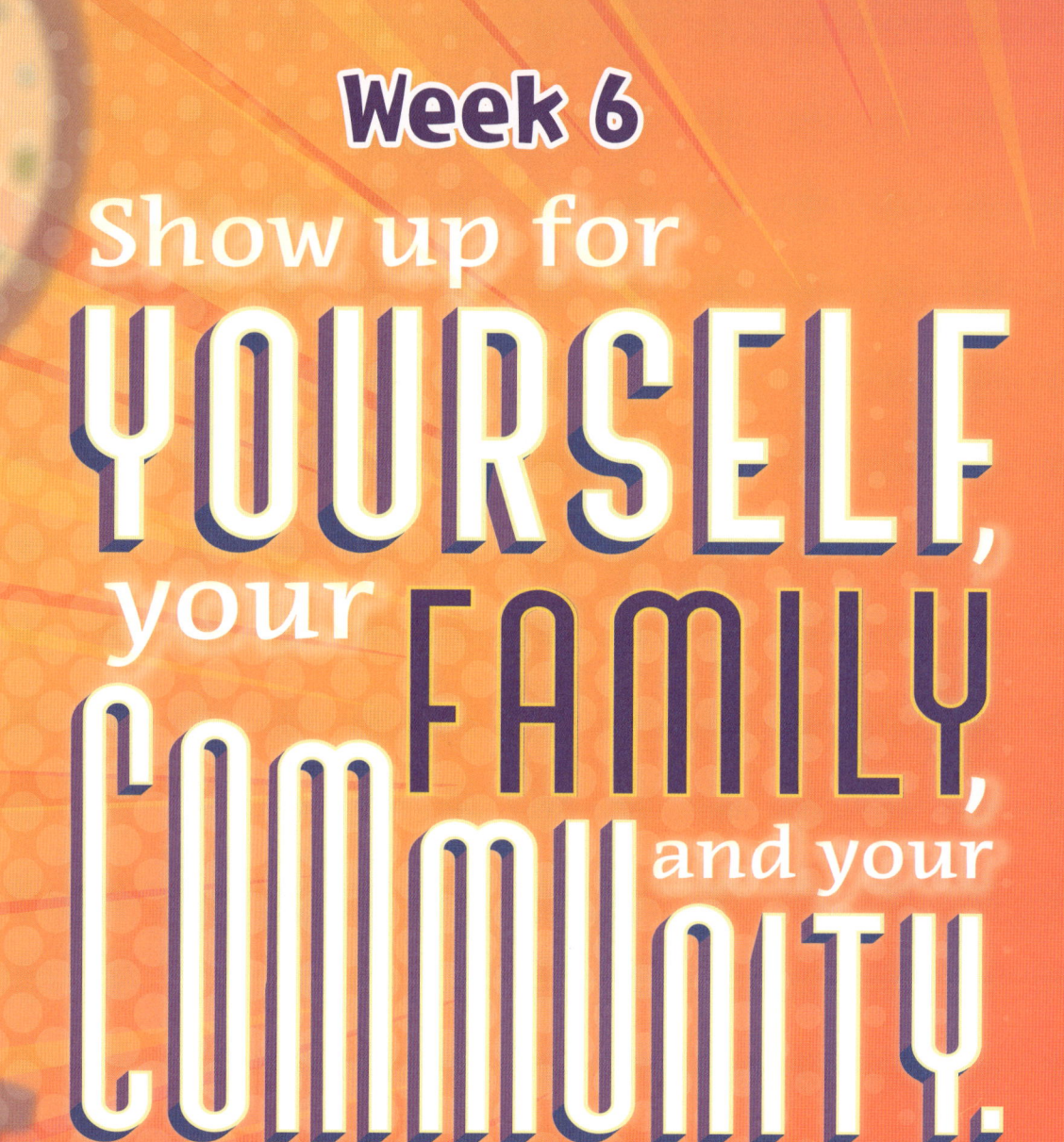

Show up for YOURSELF, your FAMILY, and your COMMUNITY.

Who am I
Victory

RESPONSIBILITY

"The way you do **ANYTHING** W

is the AY you do EVERYTHING!

— Chloé and Maud

SHOW UP FOR YOURSELF

RESPONSIBILITIES

I am **proud** of myself when I **fulfill** these **responsibilities:**

- [x]
- [ ]
- [ ]
- [ ]
- [ ]
- [ ]
- [ ]
- [ ]
- [ ]
- [ ]
- [ ]
- [ ]
- [ ]
- [ ]
- [ ]
- [ ]

Room for **improvement**!

MORE:

LESS:

GETTI
THIN

Social Media Activity: Share the steps you have taken to become more responsible.

HALFWAY MARK

Congratulations on making this far! You are **awesome**!

MUSINGS INSPIRATIONS AFFIRMAT

ONS IDEAS QUESTIONS REFLECTIONS

MUSINGS INSPIRATIONS AFFIRMAT

ONS IDEAS QUESTIONS REFLECTIONS

Week 7

DANCE!

Get Up Offa That Thing
James Brown

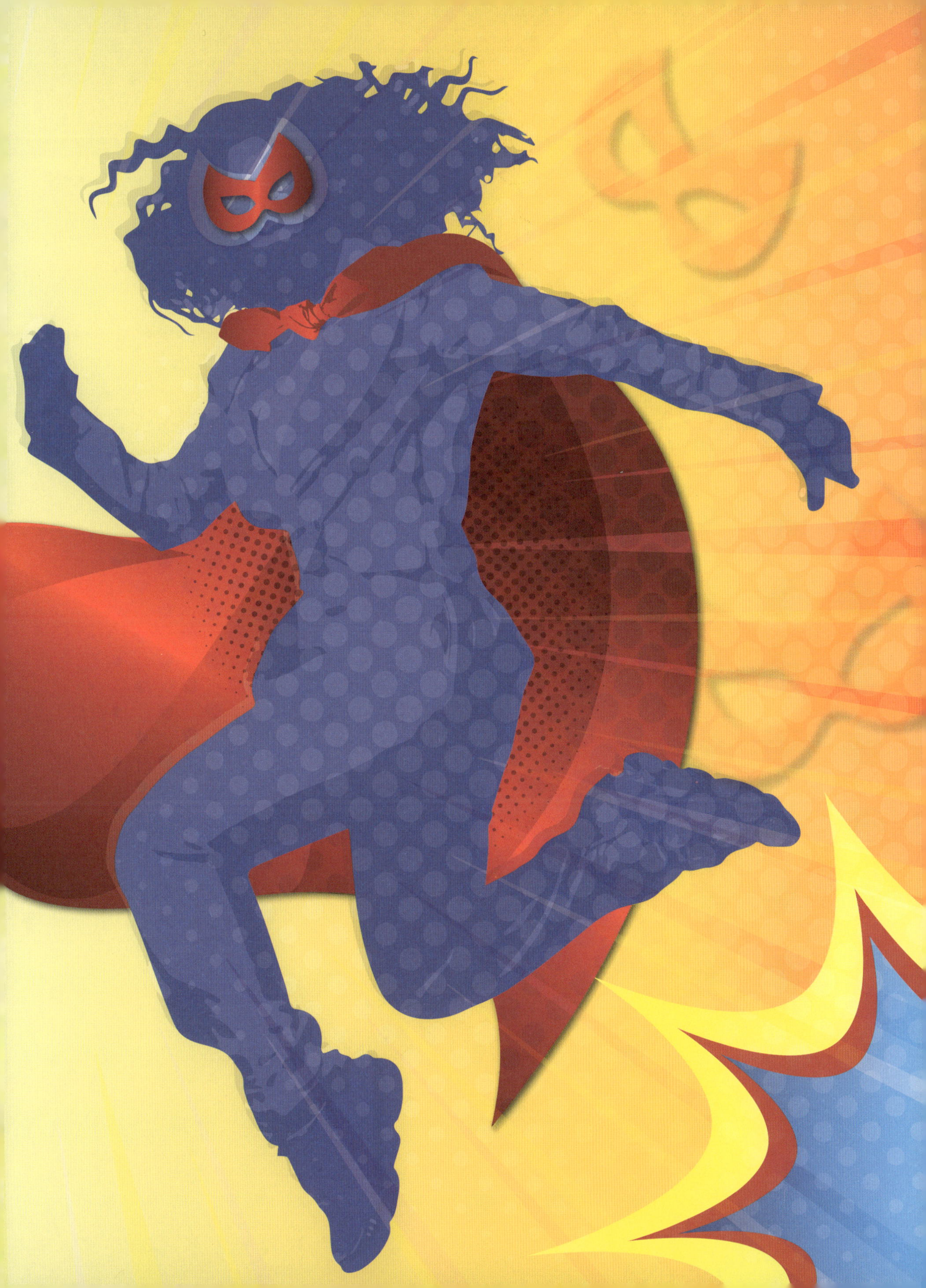

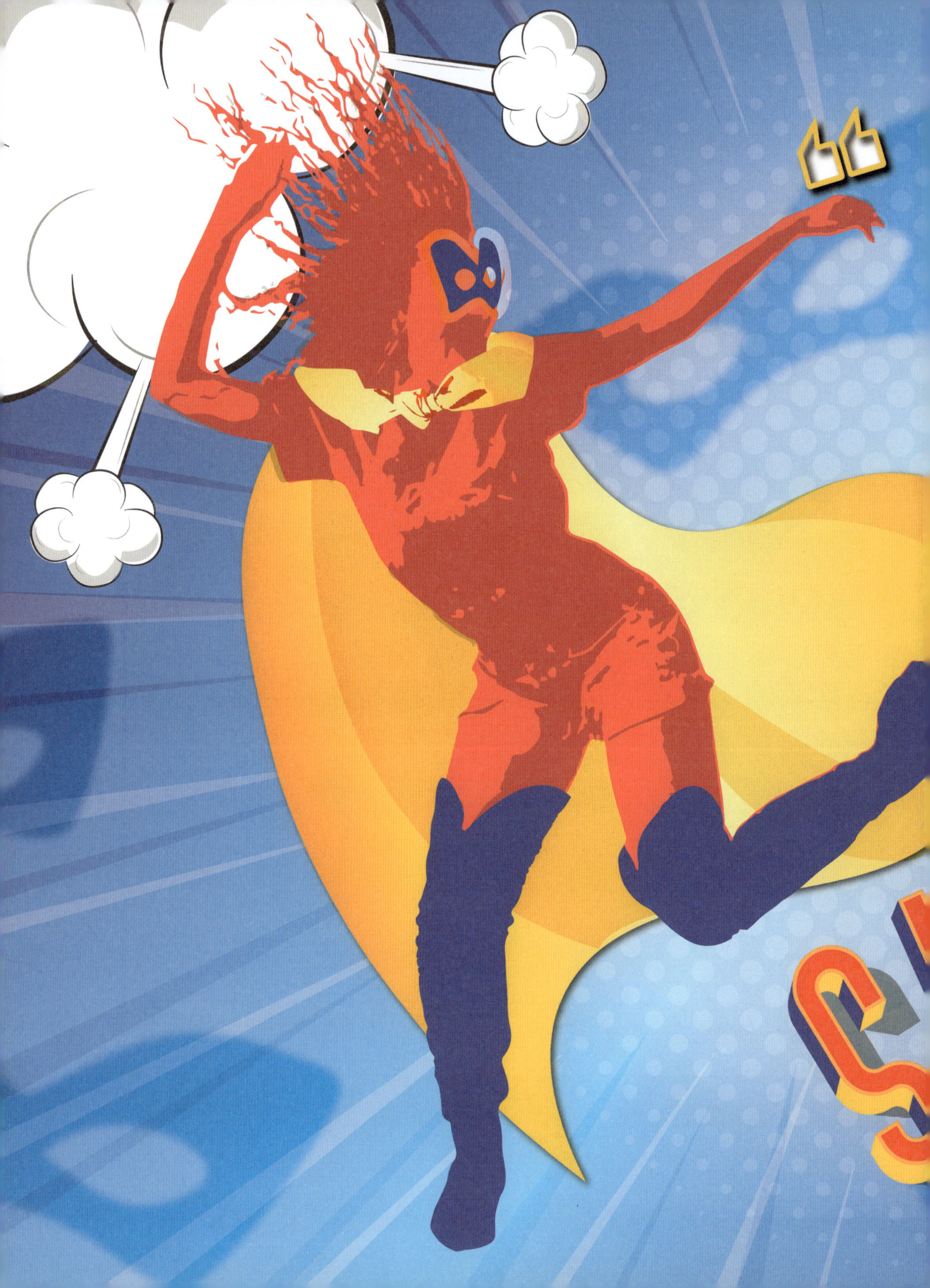

"When I express myself, I become my own Superhero!"

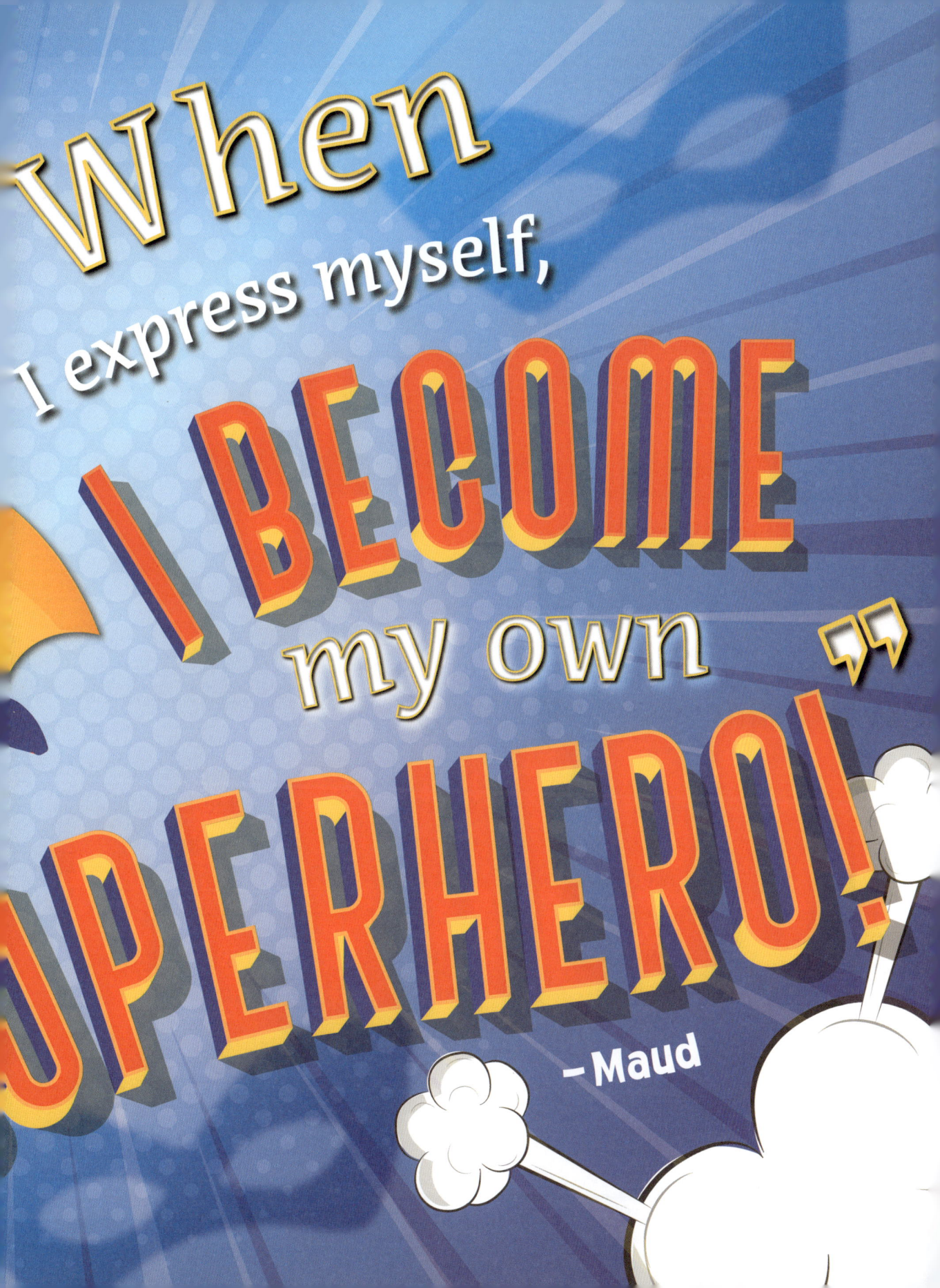

—Maud

I **dance** because:

_____
_____
_____
_____
_____
_____
_____

When I **dance**, I **feel**:

(happy)   alive   free
calm   energetic   unique
powerful   peaceful   secure
cheerful   strong   confident
accepted   wonderful   challenged
amazed   brave   comforted
fulfilled   serene   enough
                magical   universal

My **goals** as a **dancer** are:

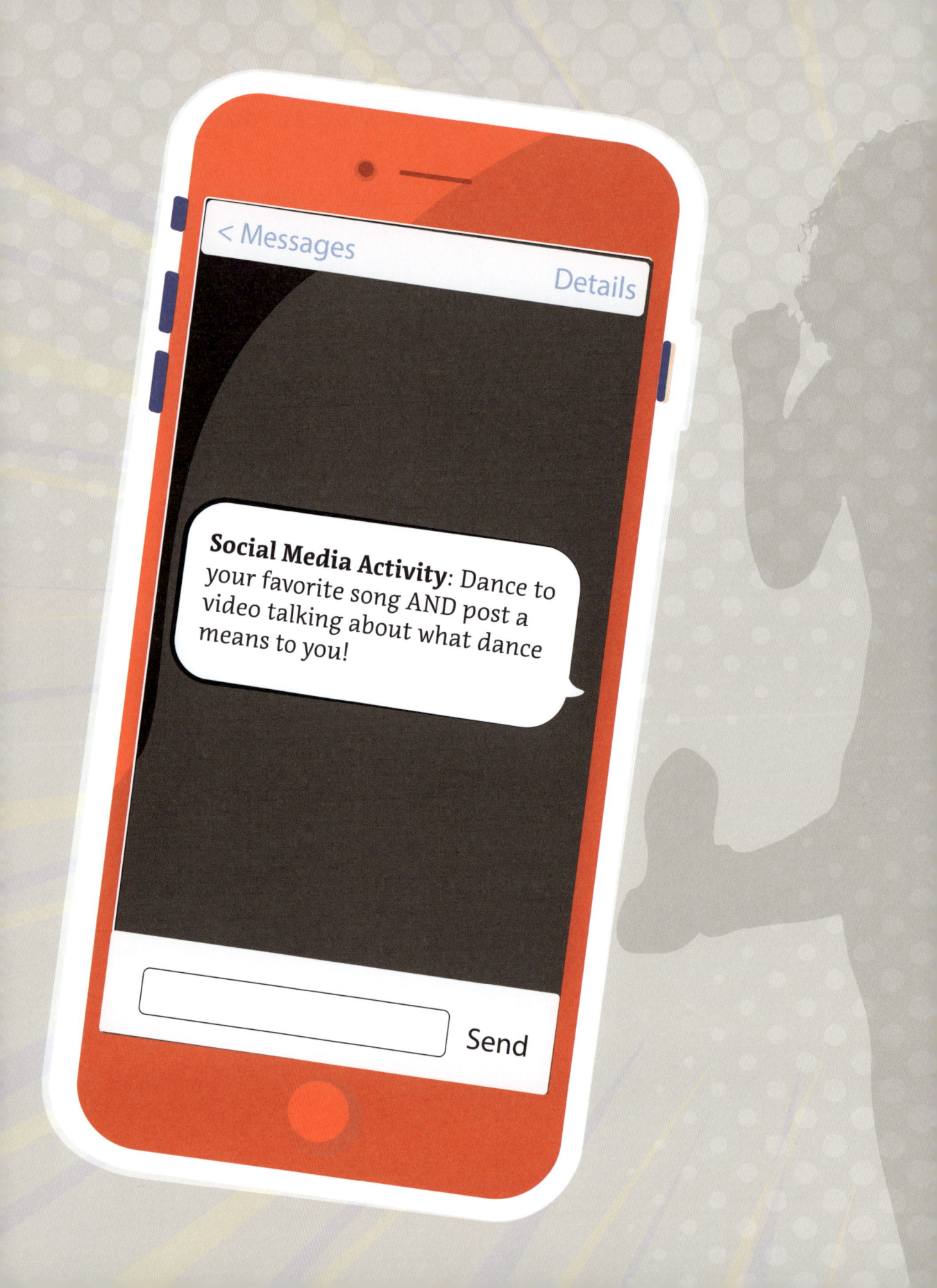

Social Media Activity: Dance to your favorite song AND post a video talking about what dance means to you!

Time to DANCE!

Express YOURSELF!

MUSINGS INSPIRATIONS AFFIRMAT

ONS IDEAS QUESTIONS REFLECTIONS

MUSINGS INSPIRATIONS AFFIRMAT

NS IDEAS QUESTIONS REFLECTIONS

Week 8

Icon
Jaden Smith

CONFIDEN

"Know your POWER, your WORTH, and your VALUES."

— Maud

I **know** I am **great** at:

I feel **confident** when I:

I want to **build** my **confidence** by:

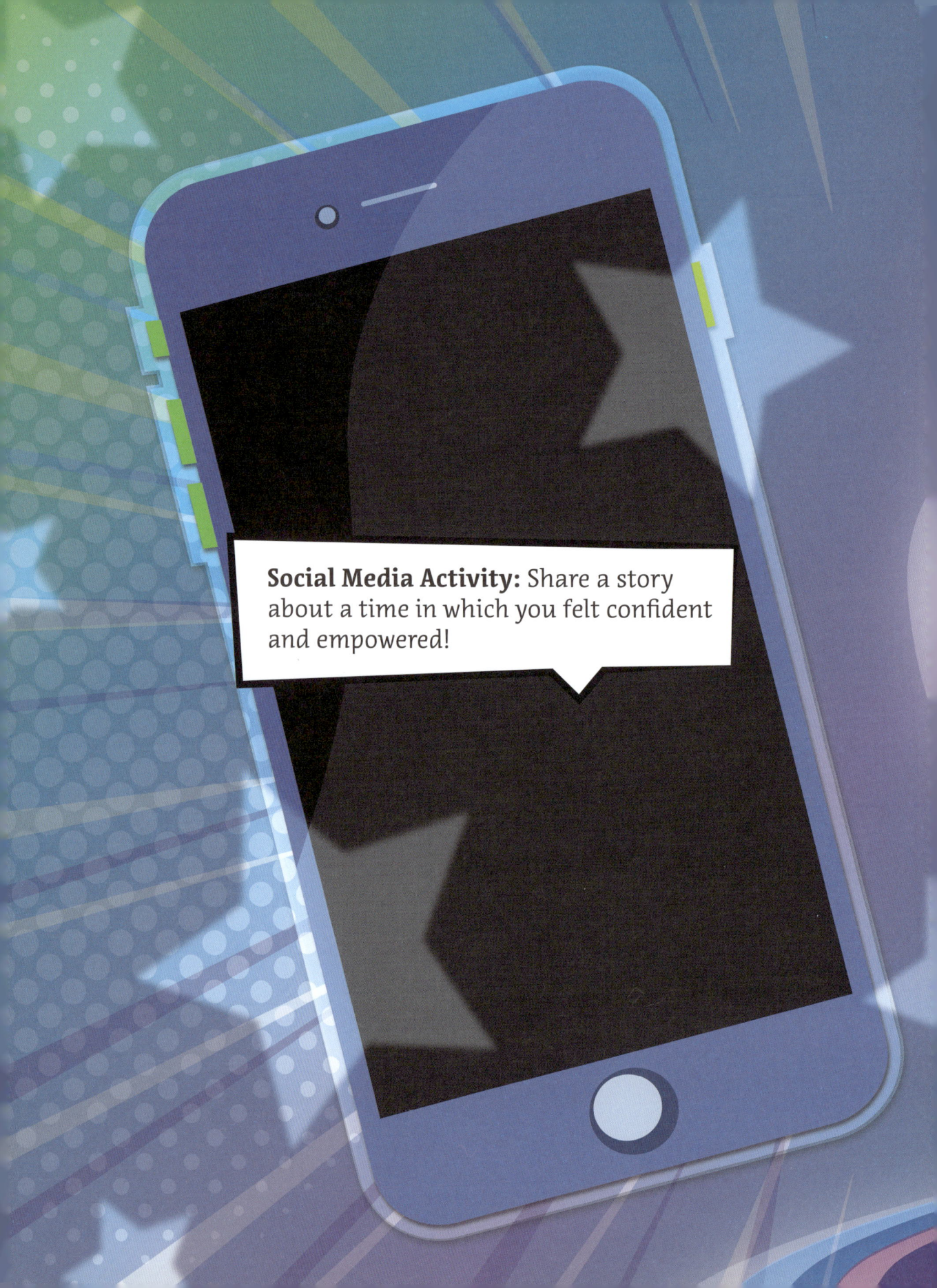

Social Media Activity: Share a story about a time in which you felt confident and empowered!

Stand in your LIGHT!

MUSINGS INSPIRATIONS AFFIRMAT

IDEAS QUESTIONS REFLECTIONS

MUSINGS INSPIRATIONS AFFIRMAT

ONS IDEAS QUESTIONS REFLECTIONS

Week 9

JEAL

"Don't hate CREATE."

— Maud

Love Yourz
J. Cole

Jealous feelings can be **natural**. It is how we **react/act** to those feelings that can **hurt** or **help** us!

When I **feel jealous**, I should:

I can **overcome** my **insecurities** by:

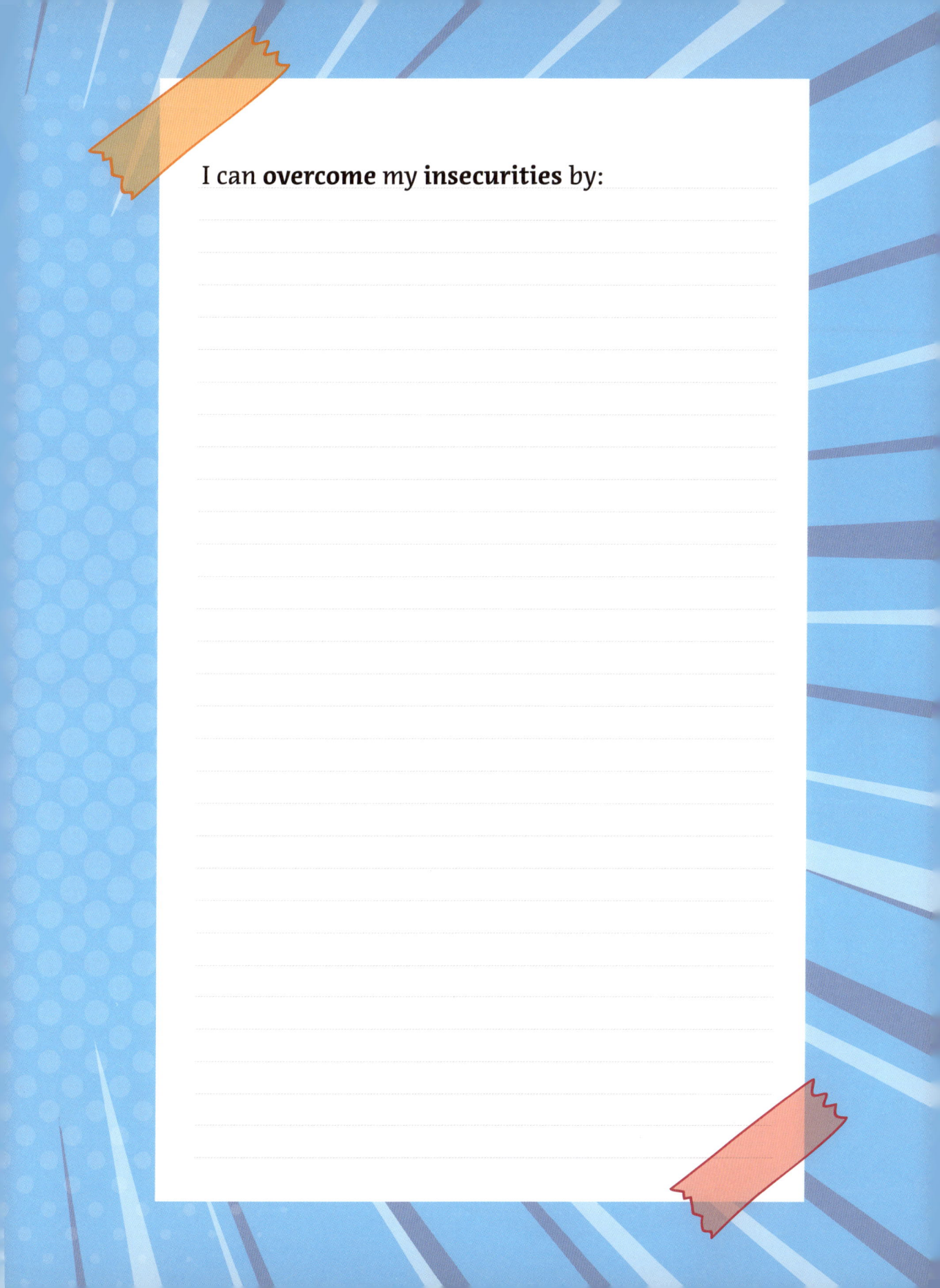

Social Media Activity: Share a time that you felt jealous and how you overcame that moment.

"Comparison is the thief of JOY."

MUSINGS INSPIRATIONS AFFIRMAT

MUSINGS INSPIRATIONS AFFIRMAT

IDEAS QUESTIONS REFLECTIONS

Week 10

WELLNESS along the JOURNEY!

Sun is Shining
Bob Marley

"DANCE TO Y

"OUR DESTINATION."
— Maud

What **Wellness** means to me:

When I'm not **feeling** well, I will reach out to:

AFFIRMATION: I AM COMMITTED TO MY WELLNESS.

To lead a **healthy** life, my **practices** are:

DAILY

WEEKLY

MONTHLY

Social Media Activity: Share your wellness and self-care practices that you do daily, weekly, and monthly.

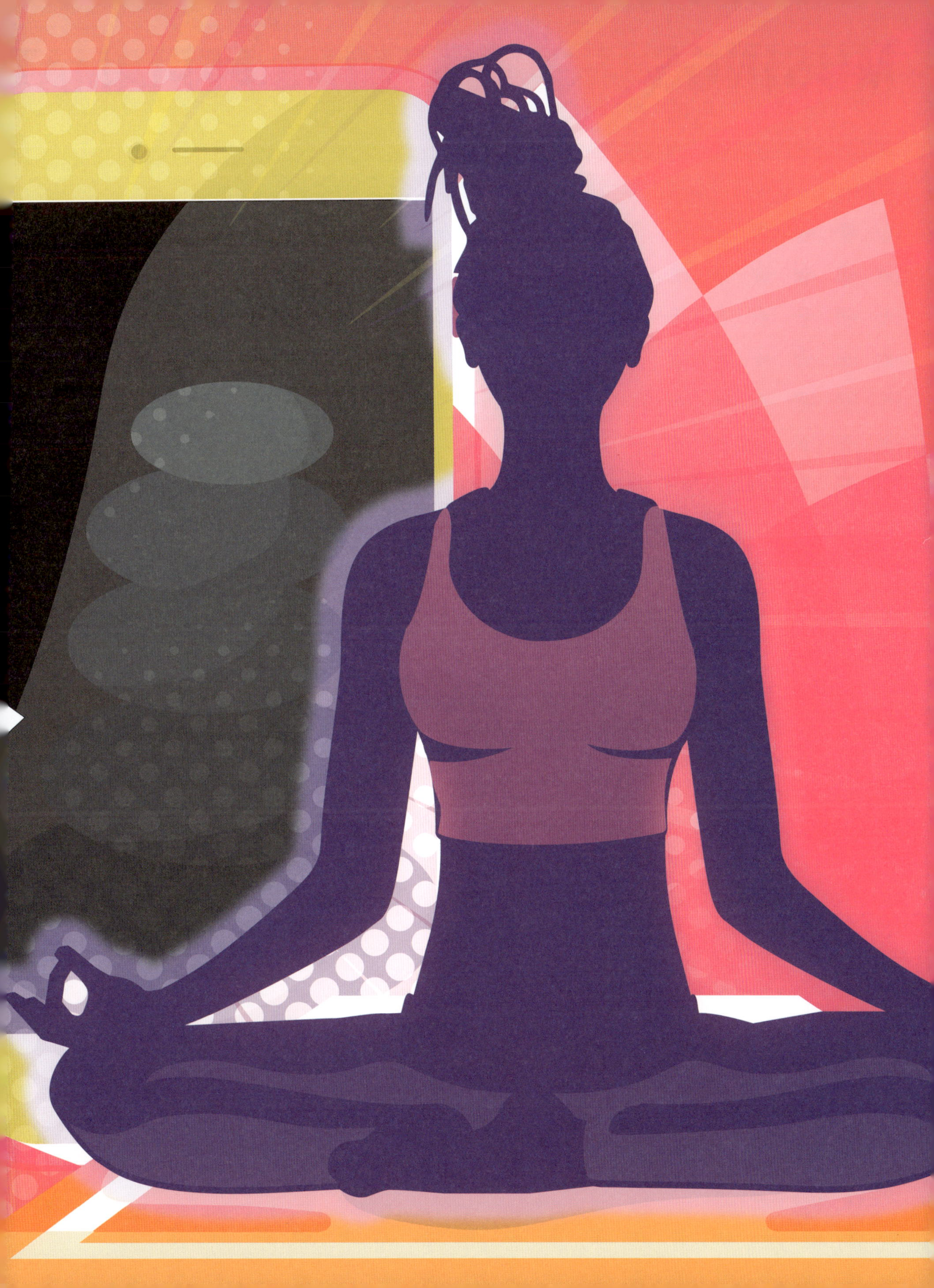

MUSINGS INSPIRATIONS AFFIRMAT

ONS IDEAS QUESTIONS REFLECTIONS

MUSINGS INSPIRATIONS AFFIRMAT

ONS IDEAS QUESTIONS REFLECTIONS

Week 11

"We are living our **DREAMS**, and continue to **DREAM FEARLESSLY!**"

– Chloé and Maud

Believe in Yourself
The Wiz

My **dreams** are:

If someone **challenges** my **dreams** I will...

Allow YOURSELF to DREAM...

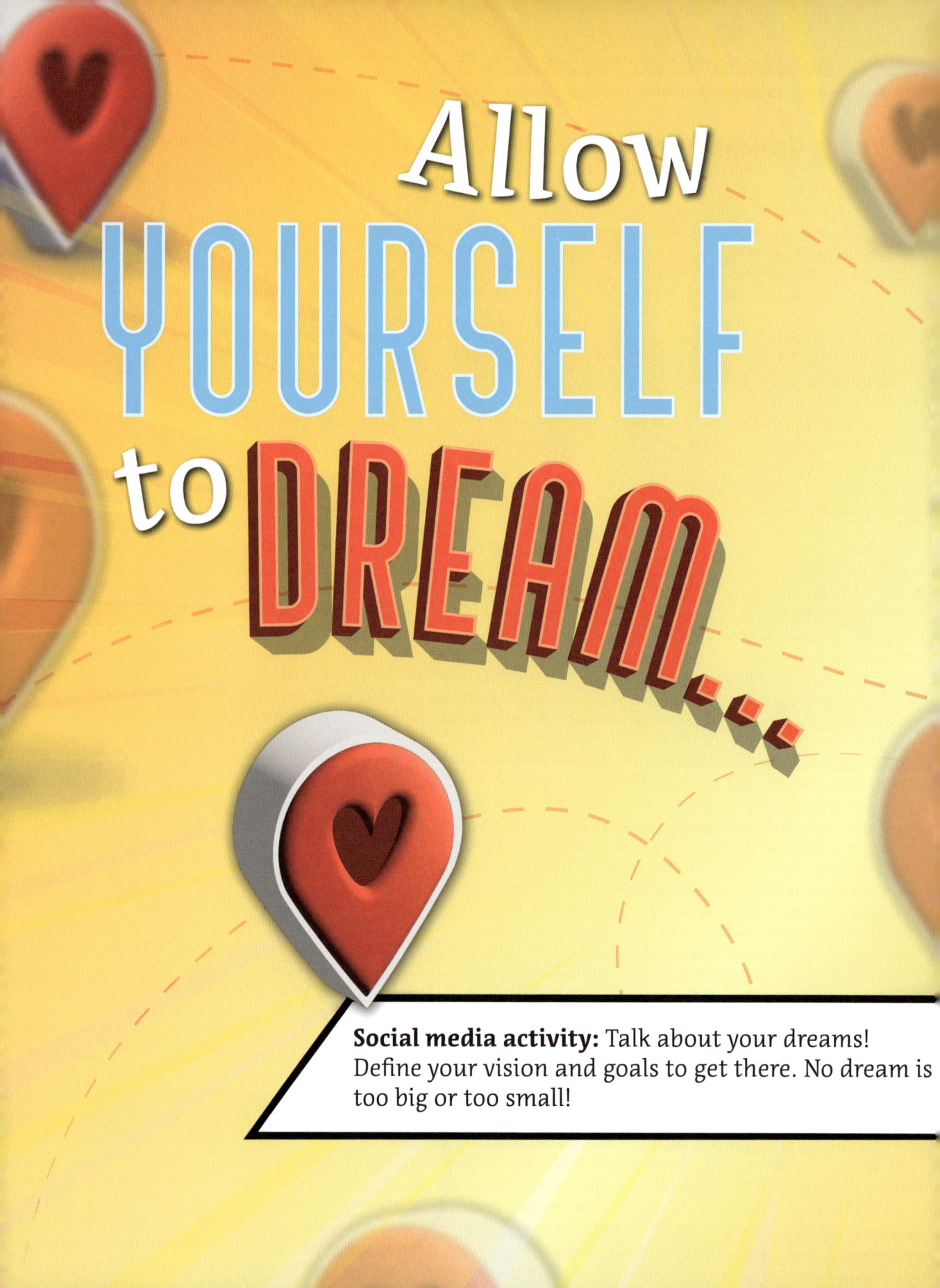

Social media activity: Talk about your dreams! Define your vision and goals to get there. No dream is too big or too small!

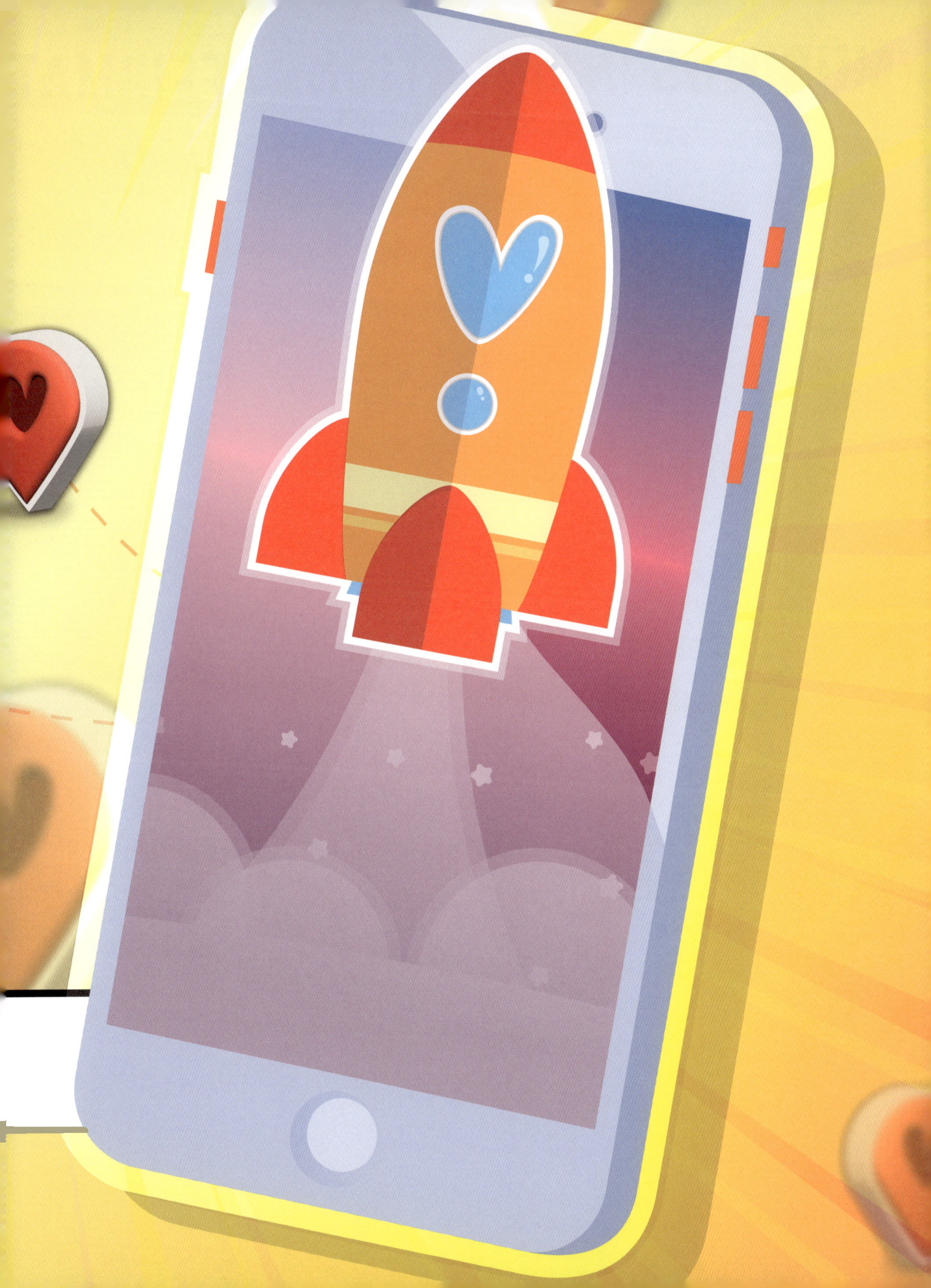

MUSINGS INSPIRATIONS AFFIRMAT

NS IDEAS QUESTIONS REFLECTIONS

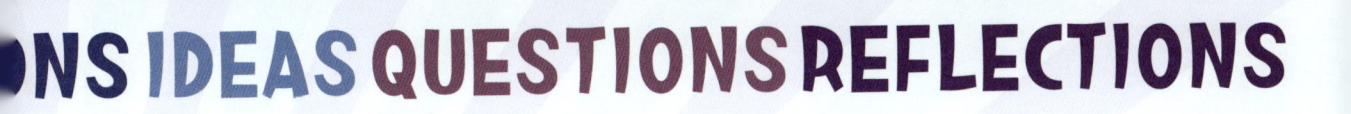

MUSINGS INSPIRATIONS AFFIRMAT

NS IDEAS QUESTIONS REFLECTIONS

Week 12

YOU MADE IT
to week 12!!!

Celebrate
Earth, Wind & Fire

"To COMMIT to YOURSELF is the true MARKER of SUCCESS!"

— Chloé and Maud

Go back and **read** your **letter** you wrote to **yourself** at the beginning of this **journey**!

How do you **feel** after **reading** your **letter**?

How have you **grown** during this **journey**?

DO NOT STOP!

Continue to **add** to your list of **gratitude**, **self-love** and **dreams**!

Be PROUD of your journey!

I AM A WINNER BECAUSE I BELIEVE IN MYSELF, AND I DO THE WORK!

Social Media Activity: Share how you feel after completing this guided journal. What did you learn? How did you grow?

MUSINGS INSPIRATIONS AFFIRMAT

ONS IDEAS QUESTIONS REFLECTIONS

MUSINGS INSPIRATIONS AFFIRMAT

ONS IDEAS QUESTIONS REFLECTIONS

MUSINGS INSPIRATIONS AFFIRMAT

IDEAS QUESTIONS REFLECTIONS